Live With Your Heart!

Don't Look Now
BUT YOUR KID IS SHOWING

Don't Look Now
BUT YOUR KID IS SHOWING

Pat Karem-Gramig

TATE PUBLISHING & *Enterprises*

Published by Tate Publishing & Enterprises, LLC
127 E. Trade Center Terrace | Mustang, Oklahoma 73064 USA
1.888.361.9473 | www.tatepublishing.com

Tate Publishing is committed to excellence in the publishing industry. The company reflects the philosophy established by the founders, based on Psalm 68:11,
"The Lord gave the word and great was the company of those who published it."

Book design copyright © 2011 by Tate Publishing, LLC. All rights reserved.
Cover design by Kellie Southerland
Interior design by Christina Hicks

Published in the United States of America

ISBN: 978-1-61777-339-6
1. Religion / Christian Life / Inspirational
2. Family & Relationships / Parenting / General
11.04.15

Dedication

James Patrick Karem was my middle child and a sight to see! He weighed nine pounds and fifteen ounces at birth. As soon as he arrived, I knew he was special—as all mothers think of their children. As he began unraveling all those special qualities about him at a very early age, I decided to record them in a book. I picked this title because it fit my Jim. In fact, it fit all my little angels. I could envision myself standing and holding a frying pan, cooking at full steam as my four little darlings' faces came peeking from behind my dress with mischievous expressions that would take on the world.

I cannot tell you how many times I attempted to write this. And each time I would tuck it away, thinking my life and my children were just as normal as anyone else's. I still have all the old drafts that I typed on onion-skinned second sheets with my old Royal typewriter.

It was in the latter sixties that I began recording Jim's shenanigans. But I just couldn't get the inspiration I needed to complete my journey. Because, you see, all mothers write about their children or their parents. It is a form of documenting our roots, and those roots are what hold our families close to our hearts.

It took the death of my son Jim to make me more aware of those bonds that we all experience with each family member: birth, love, hate (only bugs and spiders), fear, tenderness, and most of all, understanding.

This small memoir is only about his childhood; how he grew up with his brother, Brian, and his sisters, Julie and Diane. I am leaving the rest of his life to be shared at a later time by his brother, Brian. He is the more experienced writer, and his flair for the dramatic word can best describe his adulthood. I hope he will follow with a sequel.

Jim has two sons, Conner, age sixteen, and Cristian, age fifteen. Both of his boys have lived with me since August 2000. Both have Asperger's syndrome. Their father entrusted them to me since he was not able to raise them. Both Jim and his wife were dealing with their own disorders and were struggling just to be able to live a somewhat normal existence. Jim died at the age of forty-three. But there was not one day that went by that he didn't interact with his children. He loved them more than life itself. And he proved that every day of his adult life. He was a good man, and he loved totally. Anyone who knew him always talked about his constant and ever-present smile. No one knew about all the good things he did until Brian and Pastor Tuula Van Gaasbeek of the Third Lutheran Church shared those good deeds with others at his eulogy. That was Jim's gift. He did good things without recognition. He just did them because he cared.

I am dedicating this special memoir to his children, Conner and Cristian. My sincere wish is to leave them a memory of a selfless man who knew how to love: their father. I will always love you, Jim.

—Your mom.

Acknowledgments

Unfortunately, some of the people that I am about to thank were not even around professionally to help me with my son. But they are definitely a part of my life now. Without their professional guidance, my grandsons' futures would not have meaning. I am so grateful for their kind support and understanding.

Dr. Patricia Gail Williams, developmental/behavioral pediatrician

Grace Mathai, psychologist/counselor

Dr. Tato Sokhadze, PhD, assistant professor

Department of Psychiatry and Behavioral Sciences, University of Louisville

Dr. Manuel F. Casanova, professor and Kolb Endowed Chair in psychiatry and vice-chair for research at the University of Louisville

STAR Foundation (Systamatic Treatment of Autism and Related Disorder)

FEAT (Families for Effective Autism Treatment), a support group for parents with autistic children

Gerald F. Sturgeon, MD Children's Health Adolescent Medicine

Boy Scouts of America, Troop 1

Big Brothers Big Sisters of Kentuckiana

Rich Williams, Conner's Big Brother

Dominique James, Cris's Big Brother

Norman Jerome Gramig, my husband of fourteen years. I want to thank him for his support in raising my two grandsons these past ten years. I could not have done this without him. Thank you, Jerry.

And my children—Brian, Julie, and Diane, the backbone of our family. As Great-grandma Karem would say, "They are good stock!"

I wish to give one last recognition to a very special doctor I recently had the privilege to meet. His name is Peter E. Tanguay. He was the expert consultant on the film Rain Man, which starred Dustin Hoffman. I am forever grateful for his support. His credentials are far beyond the spectrum of experience. He is truly dedicated and inspires hope in all who deal with this disorder. That is why I would like to also include his credentials here. You will not be bored, only exhausted from his continuous achievements. When I wrote Dr. Tanguay about my book, he replied that there were several messages I delivered that were important, but he also stated that "most important is that every child with Asperger's Disorder should be recognized, not for his or her social deficits, but for the skills and personality characteristics that he or she excels." Thank you, Dr. Tanguay, for believing.

Autism to Asperger's:
Understanding, Diagnosing, and Treating the Rain Man Disorders

Biographical Information

Peter E. Tanguay, M.D., F.A.C. Psychiat., is the Spafford Ackerly Endowed Professor of Child and Adolescent Psychiatry (Emeritus) in the Department of Psychiatry and Behavioral Sciences, School of Medicine, University of Louisville. He is the author of many articles in leading journals on the subject of autism and has presented lectures and workshops in the United States, Europe, Japan and, most recently, in China.

From 1975 to 1985 he was Director of the NIMH-funded Child Psychiatry Clinical Research Center at UCLA. His research has focused on autism and Asperger's Disorder. It is based upon an understanding of social communication and incorporates interviews designed to assess core deficits in the condition. One goal of the work has been to develop practical ways in which teachers and clinicians can become expert in the diagnosis, understanding, and treatment of persons within the autism spectrum. Dr. Tanguay's recent publications include an invited ten-year review of Pervasive Developmental Disorder in the Journal of the American Academy of Child and Adolescent Psychiatry. In 1998 he won the Rieger Award of the American Academy of Child and Adolescent Psychiatry, as author of the most significant paper published by a child psychiatrist in the Journal of the American Academy of Child and Adolescent Psychiatry in 1997–98.

Between 1990 and 1997 Dr. Tanguay was a Director of the American Board of Psychiatry and Neurology. He is a Member of the Group for the Advancement of Psychiatry and a Fellow of the American College of Psychiatrists. He has been (2004–2010) Editor-in-Chief of the Psychiatric Residents in Training Exam (PRITE) sponsored by the American College of Psychiatrists.

He was an expert consultant on the film Rain Man, which starred Dustin Hoffman.

Table of Contents

Preface

In the late sixties, my husband, Jim, and I were in the midst of a financial struggle. We had four children, and his new job as an insurance salesman did not provide us with the income we needed to meet our family needs. It appeared the only way to supplement our income was for me to get a part-time job. So I started my search and chose only those jobs that I could arrange around our children's school schedule and those who were still at home.

One of my friends knew of my dilemma and suggested that I try modeling. At my age? Most models retired in their early twenties, and here I was almost thirty. Ridiculous! But after some thinking and research, it seemed a good possibility. I was active in some of the local theatre groups, and I thought I might try my hand at doing TV commercials. It seemed a good way to supplement income with a flexible schedule. At that time, the only way to be aware of auditions was to be a part of a modeling agency. Talent agencies did not exist in our city at that time. So I signed up and took classes. It was the agency's policy that in order to be considered for any TV commercials job assignments, I must also be willing to take as many gratis jobs as possible for the exposure and experience.

There was a mobile home show in town, and I was interviewed for the Ms. Scotchguard hostess position at one of the mobile home booths. I had to learn about fluoro chemicals and all the other amazing ingredients that Scotchguard was composed of. I got the job. And, yes, it was gratis.

One morning as I was doing my thing at the booth, a tall, slender, and mature-looking artist who wore a bright-red cape and tam approached me and asked in his Spanish accent, "Madam, would you mind if I sketched you?" I was flattered and agreed. He brought his sketching pad and easel to the booth and began drawing. As he drew, a crowd gathered to watch. He continued to ask me questions as he sketched, "What are your hobbies?" being one of them.

I replied after some thought, "I guess my favorite hobby is my children."

"How many do you have?"

"Four!"

"Oh, I see," he said as he continued on with his work. "And their ages?" he continued.

As I listed each child's name and age, it suddenly occurred to me that my Catholic background was showing. My children were chronological stepping stones, and you could tell it was inspiring the artist as he viciously continued sketching.

The crowd grew larger, and with every stroke of his pencil came chuckles. The chuckling made me wonder how he was sketching me. I finally got enough courage to ask, "You're not drawing me on a horse with no clothes on, are you?" (My hair wasn't long enough to look like Lady Godiva.)

"No." He smiled. "But you will be riding the range!"

He finished his sketch at the same time as the statement. He slowly walked up to me, smiled, and exclaimed, "It was a pleasure, madam!" I accepted his sketch of me and started smiling just like the crowd that gathered around him. He had me riding the range, all right! But, in my kitchen surrounded by a kitchen range, pots and pans and a diapered child! Just as you see me on the next page.

Prologue

Seasons

Peace fell upon the earth and man
had his way with Nature.
He took the gentleness of the
morning rain and embraced it
with the seed. A subtle hint of life
came forth and introduced
us to spring.

The life took root and shared its
love and beauty among all men.
With great abundance, the seed
blossomed all through the season of
summer.

Each precious seed was then sowed
and harvested by man. And when he
finished his long and rigorous
chore, bowed his head in gratitude,
closing life's chapter to fall.

So man rested now, sharing the fruits
of his labor that would carry him
through the bitter, cold days of winter.

Seasons carry us through life's journey.
Taking care to be kind to those
who sowed life's seed with caring in
hopes that each of us would gather
once again in the spring.

—Pat Karem Gramig

Cast of Characters

The Karem Gang: Brian, Jim Pat, Julie, Diane

The Kid Behind the Bars:
James Patrick Karem

A Star Is Born

My husband and I were having difficulty naming our third child. We just couldn't decide what suited this fine, strapping young man who weighed in at nine pounds and fifteen ounces. He came into this world almost as an adult. Too big for just formula feedings, he had to have steak and potatoes. Since he had no teeth as yet, I scaled it down to cereal and formula. That seemed to satisfy his insatiable appetite—at least at the time.

But it took his Lebanese grandfather, Fred Karem, to properly name him.

"Why don't you name him James Patrick?" he suggested. "James, after his father, and Patrick (the masculine form of Patricia) after his mother?"

His father and I both agreed. Now can you imagine this great Irish name that was placed on a child with Lebanese/Russian heritage? That only proved how special he was!

Because of his size at birth and his appetite, Jim Pat got a few reputations. I was also responsible for his nickname, "Hoss," after Hoss Cartwright from the TV series Bonanza. Jim seemed to fit that role perfectly. I even noted it in his baby book: Hoss will grow up to be a big man! And so he would continue on that path.

As Jim grew older and people were aware that he had a problem, they would awkwardly inquire about it. I would look them straight in the eye and reply distinctly and in a tense monotone, "My son was born with his umbilical cord attached to the refrigerator!" Well, that lightened up the moment, and once they realized I was joking, we moved on to a more comfortable conversation.

His early years were really not as exciting, as I recall. He just ate and slept as most babies do. Jim mostly ate. He didn't start creating pandemonium until he outgrew his playpen. Then panic became his middle name.

Jim was about three years old, and it was a beautiful summer morning. We had a small vegetable garden my son Brian had planted next to their swing set. I went outside to pick some pole beans for dinner. Jim wanted to come along. I encouraged him to stay in the house, that I would only be a minute. He insisted. I insisted even more. Of course, I won. Jim didn't like that at all, but he stayed. I finished collecting the beans I needed and started into the house. As I pushed the door to enter, it wouldn't budge. I pushed again. It stayed shut. I panicked, for Jim was alone in the house. He had a plan, and I wasn't a part of it.

The door had glass panes at the top, and as I peeked into the kitchen area, I could see these two big brown eyes staring back at me with a determined look, a look of revenge. I tried pleading, begging, sweet-talking, and finally, threatening. Nothing worked. He only stared back at me with this determined look that he was going to get his way. And then he disappeared.

"Jim Pat, honey! Let Mommy in, please. Jim, honey, open the door, and let me in."

Absolute silence. No Jim Pat. I had to do something, so I started searching each window for one that hopefully was unlocked. I found one. The bathroom window was cracked open slightly, and I could easily undo the screen. As I carefully climbed in, I happened to glance over my shoulder to witness an audience of neighbors encouraging me to do the right thing. And that was not to step into an open toilet. Once I was in the house, I just looked at my determined child, too angry and too grateful that he was safe. Jim just stood there by his record player and mischievously smiled at me.

"Mean ol' Mom!" he declared. That statement became Jim's nickname for me whenever he didn't get his way.

Runaway to Church Child

There was this time Jim Pat was determined to go to church with his dad. Since our kids were still quite small, we took them to church as a family but not every Sunday. We didn't think God would even be ready for our Lebanese gang. One of us would babysit while the other was able to go to church in peace. We always took turns. Why? Well, whenever we tried to go as a family, something always occurred out of the ordinary. Like when Diane, who was in training pants, decided she didn't want to wear any underwear to church. Of course, we didn't know that…until my husband picked her up and felt a bare bottom.

"Pat, Diane isn't wearing any pants!" he gasped. The priest overheard this declaration since we were in the first pew. A slight grin covered his face while continuing with the Mass.

All my kids were individuals, which is good except when it gets in the way of good behavior.

Jim Pat was a very stubborn child. When Jim Pat got something in his mind, it was hard for anyone to change it. He had to do what he set out to do. And this time it was going to church with his father. His dad had finally convinced him to stay home with me…he thought. As he drove away to Mass, I sat down at our little Spinet piano to play some of Jim Pat's favorite music pieces, thinking this would calm him down and get his mind off of going to church. There I was, playing and singing and not paying a bit of attention to what the Lebanese lion was up to. I looked over to give him a big smile. I smiled at nobody. Jim Pat was gone. I panicked.

"Lord, where did he go now? Jim Pat, answer me!"

No Jim Pat. I started looking in all his favorite hiding places. Not in the closet, not in the bathroom, not under his bed or near the refrigerator. I began an all-out search in the neighborhood. The neighborhood kids joined in by riding their bikes through the neighborhood streets. I started imagining all kinds of things that could be happening to my little baby. What if he had been kidnapped or struck down by a car and left for dead? These are all the things a mother worries about when her child is not in her immediate grasp.

My husband finally arrived back from church, and I told him what happened. We put Brian and Julie in the car and started circling the neighborhood. Surely someone would notice a wandering child and know he was lost. As we turned the corner, we noticed a car following behind us, trying to get us to stop.

"Jim, pull over," I said.

As we pulled over, two teenage girls pulled alongside and asked if we were looking for a little boy.

"Oh, yes!" I shouted.

"Follow us," they said.

Exactly one block over from where we lived, we pulled up in the driveway. I leaped out of the car and dashed for the door. A young woman met me with a friendly greeting of, "Hi, are you Henry's mother?"

I stood there, stunned. *Oh, Lord, I found the wrong kid*, I thought.

"I beg your pardon? No, I am Jim Pat Karem's mother."

I started describing my son in great detail when out popped Jim Pat around the kitchen door, beaming from ear to ear with a Hostess Twinkie in one hand and more of it all over his face.

"Hi, Mom!" He grinned.

It seemed when my son decided to go out on his adventure to church, he had taken an alias. His favorite cartoon character in the funny papers was Henry, a small bald-headed child who always got himself into trouble. How appropriate of my son to choose this name. It certainly captured my son's character.

I picked up my "Henry," gave him a squeeze, and thanked my neighbor for keeping him safe.

The Music Man

Jim Pat loved music. He had a record player that Santa Claus brought him one year with a complete set of Walt Disney records. We even bought him the record "You're a Good Man, Charlie Brown" from the Peanuts gang. The Peanuts gang kind of resembled my gang a little too, I think. My guy would pass the time away playing those records constantly and rocking back and forth to each and every tune. He knew every one by heart and would recite along with each, especially the Charlie Brown record. Whenever we took the kids for a Sunday afternoon ride, Jim would sit in the back and recite every word from every character. He would do the exact inflections of each conversation. He would cup his hand up to his ear and make the noises that represented the voices of the adults (bwa bwy bwa bwy bwa bwy bwa bwy bwy bwy) to a very steady tune. It was almost identical to the Charlie Brown recording.

Then was the unforgettable day when he broke his favorite toy, the record player. He was devastated and couldn't wait to tell me how much he wanted us to get it fixed. He broke it on a Sunday morning, and back then when all stores were closed on Sundays. That was the Lord's Day, the day of "thou shalt not make a profit." We tried to explain to him that we would get his record player fixed the very next day and first thing. This was not good enough. Jim wanted it fixed now.

So with great determination and speed and without anyone noticing, Jim grabbed his record player, grabbed my husband's keys, and darted for the car. He threw the record player in the backseat, jumped in the front seat, put the car in reverse, and slowly drove out of the driveway, across the street, and hit the curb.

While all this is going on, Jim was looking at me with that determined look, yelling at the top of his voice, "I want my record player fixed! I want my record player fixed!"

The car stopped, Jim Pat stopped yelling, and my heart was put on pause.

A Hairy Experience

My life was never boring, and the challenges that came my way were even more exciting. Jim Pat was my challenge. To outthink him was impossible. This child could outmaneuver an army general in wartime. He was always challenged by his determination.

After dinner, I would let the kids go back outside and play if it was summer and the days were long. If it was winter, they would watch a little TV or play in their rooms or downstairs in our finished basement.

That was when I would have my time to read the newspaper, usually at the dinner table. My mistake. I had Jim Pat checking in and asking me to do this or asking me to do that or wanting me to do this or wanting me to do that. The word no was not in his vocabulary of acceptance.

This particular evening, after the dishes were washed and put away, I sat down at the table to do the crossword puzzle. Jim Pat couldn't stand seeing me be quiet. So he pestered me with his usual questions. His requests were unreasonable, so I politely said, "No, Jim Pat. The answer is no!"

He seemed to accept my answer and left the room. I continued to work on my puzzle. Shortly, Jim came back into the room, raised his hand holding a pair of scissors, and started hacking off my long blonde hair.

"You mean mom!" he yelled and stomped out of the room on his tiptoes. He seemed to have conquered the conqueror with one swift snip of the scissors.

I was in total shock! He cut me to the quick…literally! I couldn't figure out if he was just trying to get his way with his dramatic barbering, or if he was turning into some sort of Frankenstein. I didn't have a clue. But I did know from past experience that if I pursued this issue with him now it might develop into a temper outburst that I was not prepared to deal with at the time. So I backed off. I let it go. As I sat there still stunned by it all, I began to snicker and then slowly chuckle. I couldn't help seeing the humor in this, even though I now had a hairstyle that would freak out Vampira. I didn't look normal again for a long time. It was only after my hair grew back that I discovered that my sense of humor saved us both that day.

Travelin' Man

My husband started a new job as a pharmaceutical salesman that took him out of town frequently. We lived in a one-floor house at the time. The kids were small. I had Brian in training pants, and Julie and Jim were still in diapers. Diane, my youngest, had not arrived on the scene yet.

It was a crisp fall day, and Jim was on the road. I was home alone with three kids, who all had colds and slight fevers. It seemed that no matter where I turned there was a sniffling child hanging on to me, crying to be held or telling me something was hurting through a wail of tears. I was trying to attend to them, do laundry, a little house cleaning, as well as prepare dinner. I was not accomplishing any of this as my three little ones hung onto my skirt, crying and sniffling and each wanting me to hold them. Finally, I had had it.

My patience was really raw now, and I prayed that their father better come home soon. I needed relief. I caught sight of a towel, and then I caught sight of my walk-in pantry.

"Oh, Lord, I sure hope this works," I sighed.

I gained all the power I could muster, grabbed the towel, and made a break for the pantry. I knew I would be safe in there. But right behind me ran the three little horsemen, and they were closing in on me.

"Daddy's home!" I yelled as I ran for the pantry.

All three headed for the front door. Lady, our beagle, raised her head in a piercing howl and charged under the bed (she didn't like my husband at all, and that's where she hid when he arrived home). I made my escape. Inside the pantry, I took my trusty towel and shoved it in my face and screamed and screamed and screamed.

When I stopped, I could hear the pitter patter of tiny feet rushing toward the pantry.

"Mommy! We can't find Daddy! Mommy, whatcha doin'? Mommy, I'm hungry! Mommy, my head hurts!"

One more scream was left inside me, and I had to let it out. "Aaahh!"

It felt so good. Then with total calm and control, I slowly opened the pantry door and forced a smile onto my face.

"Hi, Mommy! Whatcha doin' in the pantry, Mommy?"

"Looking for your father, dear."

I grabbed the towel, strutted toward the dirty clothes hamper like a fashion model, dumped the remains of the towel, and then started dinner. So much for stress relief. My pantry became my constant companion. So did the towel.

Temper, Temper

As the children grew older, we set up some rules and responsibilities for each of them. They were simple ones that gave them responsibility and reward. I made a poster with each child's name listing the chores they had to do in order to receive their weekly allowance: clean your room, make your bed, pick up your toys, feed the dog, etc.

I always told the children that if I asked them to pick up their toys and they didn't, they might find that toy missing. I never told them what I did with the toys. I would usually hide it from them for a while, and when I thought they had earned it back, the toys would mysteriously show up, sometimes under the Christmas tree. Santa never got the blame, but he always got the credit for being so generous by returning their toy. I thought this was a much better idea than a bag of switches from Santa that I always got threatened with when my parents thought I was bad.

Jim Pat didn't like rules. He would reluctantly obey but always with a grunt or a groan. He was cleaning up his room one day and asked to go outside and play. I agreed that he could, but he had to put away his football first, which he still had lying on the bedroom floor.

He said, "Okay, Mom." So I left his room. Jim Pat went outside, and I continued my chores. As I was vacuuming down the hall next to Jim Pat's room, I noticed his football still lying against his bed. I picked it up and put it in the front hall closet for safekeeping and to teach Jim a lesson.

Later that day, Jim came in the house from playing and immediately ran to his room.

"Where's my football?" he shouted.

"Did you put it away like I asked you?"

He started rooting through his toy box in the closet and searched angrily for it.

"Where's my football?"

And then, like a tornado ripping through a town, Jim began to stomp through his room, tear down his bedclothes, and throw his pillows on the floor while ranting like a mad bull. I just stood by and watched. After a while, he ran out of steam and calmed down, still huffing and puffing away. I looked at him long and hard, and then I asked him one simple question: "Are you done now?"

"Yes!" he yelled.

"Good," I replied. "Now clean up your room, and you don't leave here till you do."

He gave me the "mean mom" look, started picking up his mess, and replied, "All right" in a very sing-songy tone.

Later that week, he got his football back. I didn't have the heart to have him wait until Christmas.

School Days

I registered Jim Pat in kindergarten at St. Pius School. Their kindergarten teacher was wonderful. Brian and Julie loved her. She related well to the children and had a lot of patience with them. I should know. I substituted for her one morning, and when she returned later that day, I went home with a migraine.

I asked her to do me a favor and observe Jim Pat. I was certain he had some sort of disability, but I needed an expert's opinion. She did just that. When she called me in to her office a couple of weeks later, she gave me her observations.

"Jim Pat is very bright, Pat. But he has a coordination problem. He also walks on his tiptoes and plays imaginary baseball with his fingers. He sometimes is off to himself and does not relate well with the other children. I think a good physical examination is in order."

I contacted our family doctor, and the search began. After the complete physical, our doctor determined that he was very healthy, but I needed to contact a neurologist for further findings. After that examination, the neurologist explained more completely about Jim. He explained it in pretty simple terms: "Jim was born with some damage done to his nervous system. It's like a frayed telephone wire. Jim's brain sends out messages to his body. If he wants to jump rope, his brain sends that message out to that part of the body, his legs. But because of the frayed wiring in his nervous system, other parts of the body receive the message as well. This causes his coordination problem."

The doctor also diagnosed Jim Pat as hyperactive. Back when Jim was a baby, they knew very little about ADHD or autism.

The doctor was encouraging and said that Jim was like a lot of other children and adults who have this problem. He explained that they just learn to the tune of a different drummer. He also explained that society has placed rules on our levels of learning, and some of us just don't learn in that structured way. Jim was one of these people. He also mentioned that it would take time, patience, and lots of understanding to help Jim manage through his life. Jim was placed on Ritalin for his hyper-activity, and family counseling was also suggested. He still had his unique conversations with himself, walked on his tiptoes, and still played imaginary baseball with his fingers. But I didn't care. Once he began taking his medication, Jim was able to go to school and focus better than he ever had. That meant he would be able to learn with the rest of his classmates without causing disruption. Jim was beginning to make some positive progress at last.

Counseling Can Be Fun

Per the doctor's recommendation, we set up weekly sessions through the Child Guidance Clinic. Jim Pat's therapist was a wonderful middle-aged woman. She was our angel from heaven. She was patient, kind, and very understanding. She never told us what we needed to do; she only listened and offered us options. It was up to us to make our final decision.

Jim Pat liked her a lot. She would play games with him. Sometimes he would win, and sometimes he would lose. She was trying to teach him that it was okay to lose sometimes. No one was perfect. It was hard for him to realize this because of his determination to do everything perfectly. These weekly sessions were a great support system for my son. And he gave it his best every time.

Another support system was the family counseling sessions. Parents were encouraged to attend sessions like this in order to continue the therapy that was being given to their child at the guidance clinic. My husband and I attended these sessions together for a while. Then my husband refused to attend with me. He claimed he didn't need them.

We were having marital problems at that time, as well as our struggle with finances. We also added a fourth addition to the family, Diane. We were beginning to feel the strain on our marriage more each day.

Jim Pat and the other children were being strongly affected by our marital problems. So now all of us were attending the weekly family counseling sessions. Jim Pat was still seeing his personal counselor.

One day, I approached her and told her that I was so sorry my husband refused to join us. She told me that you couldn't force someone to do anything; it had to be his decision. I also told her we were not getting along and I was seriously considering divorce. I felt that the emotional stability of the children and I were at risk in this no-win marriage, and I hesitated to make any kind of rash decision. And I was also Catholic, and divorce would be against the rules of the church.

Pat Karem–Gramig

She hesitated for a bit and then replied, "Pat, I can't tell you what to do. That is your decision. But I can tell you this. You have four children to raise. You do not need a fifth." She had given me my answer.

It took over a year of legal separation before the divorce was final. It was a rough year on all of us, but we eventually adjusted to a new life, including my former husband. In fact, he was relieved that he could continue his life the way he wanted. He eventually remarried, and I moved on to find full-time employment.

My four Lebanese tigers and I continued our weekly family counseling sessions together. We were actually looking forward to them, and each of us seemed to be happy about our progress.

After one of these sessions, our counselor informed me that they wanted to video tape us during a session and also wanted my consent for us to be observed by other staff members behind a one-way mirror. They didn't want me to let the children know so they would be more spontaneous. I was told if I was uncomfortable with this, they would not do it. I looked around at my kids, took a look at the counselor, and started chuckling to myself.

He really doesn't know what he is getting himself into with my group, I thought. So I agreed. *Let the games begin!* I shouted to myself. I could hardly wait to see how this was going to turn out.

The following week, they took us to a large room and asked us to sit and wait. Kids just don't sit and wait. They have to be moving. My oldest son, Brian, walked over to the huge one-way mirror and then walked over to me.

"Mom?" he asked. "Are there people behind that mirror?"

"Why do you think that, Brian?" I answered.

"Well, I just saw someone light up a cigarette, and I could see them back there!"

I couldn't wait to tell. My son Brian, the genius, figured out the plan. When I told the counselor that my children discovered the secret behind the one-way mirror, he discussed it with all four and asked them if they would object to having other counselors observe them. They had no problem with that. The session began, and each of us was so wrapped up in our discussions that we forgot about the video and the mirror.

After the session was over, our counselor asked us if we would like to meet the people behind the mirror. We all said yes.

As each member filed out, they mingled. One lady approached me and claimed with a big smile on her face, "Mrs. Karem, I just wanted to let you know, you have a very unique family." Her grin remained on her face as if to signify that we were special. I already knew that.

Other Church Stories

Our family life changed dramatically after I got divorced. I took a job as a promotion director at a new shopping center. A lot of adjustments had to be made, and we all were giving it our best. I was tired a lot more, and I became a much more organized person. But we were making progress.

Jim Pat was still trying hard to overcome many obstacles in his life. One thing in particular was that Jim found it difficult to show much affection. He didn't like for people to hug him or touch him much. But a day didn't go by that I didn't hug him or kiss him or tell him how much I loved him. Finally, I received my reward.

One summer Sunday, I took the kids to the cathedral downtown for the evening Mass. It was hot and muggy, and we were all too tired to attend an early Mass that day. We were all kneeling quietly during the Consecration of the Mass, and Jim Pat looked up at me and with a very loud but gentle voice proclaimed before God and everybody, "I love you, Mom."

"I love you too, Jim Pat." Nothing else needed to be said. I just kissed him before God and the congregation.

All of us loved going to Mass at the cathedral. It was a beautiful, old church. They were undergoing a renovation, and the air conditioning was not working very well. When we returned several weeks later to attend another evening Mass, it seemed even hotter than it was before. But we prayed through it. The children began to tire and fidget during the priest's sermon. He seemed to talk on endlessly, and the more he talked, the more tired and fidgety they became.

The priest finally finished his sermon and blessed the congregation. As he started to leave the pulpit, a loud ring of applause could be heard from the back of the church. I turned with a startled look and saw Jim Pat clapping his hands.

I haven't figured out yet whether Jim was applauding him because he finally finished or because he gave such a wonderful sermon. All I know is that the full attention of the congregation focused on my family and was giving very harsh glances our way. Except the priest. He continued his walk back to the altar with a very slight devilish grin. I think he was longing to do an encore.

More School Stuff

Brian, Julie, and Jim were now attending Goldsmith Elementary. St Pius eliminated the first grade, and when I had to put Jim Pat at Goldsmith, I put them all there. Actually, if I had not done so, I would not have had the counseling opportunities for my family. They continued testing Jim every year. The principal at Goldsmith was well liked by everyone. She was a kind and fair person.

The mothers in the neighborhood took turns carpooling, and I quickly earned the title "Curb Karem." I had a station wagon, and when it was my turn, it was like driving a school bus full of kids. So my aim wasn't all that good when I turned the corners of any street. I usually clipped a curb with my tires and bumped my way over it. Thus, "Curb Karem" came into existence.

I liked my new name. It made me feel like Zorro. Except the State of Kentucky wouldn't allow me to wear a mask to hide my identity.

My daughter Diane had not started school yet. So when it was my turn to pick the children up, I would bring a book to read to her as we waited for school dismissal. Her favorite story was from the Uncle Remus stories, "Brer Rabbit and the Briar Patch." I loved taking on the different voices and playing out the role of each character. It was great fun passing the time away with her while we waited for our group.

One day, I got a call from the school principal. She wanted me to come to a conference that day with her and Jim Pat's teacher. It seemed Jim was having some difficulty relating to her. He was being disruptive in class, talking when he shouldn't, and entertaining himself with other things outside the school criteria. As I mentioned before, this was Jim and his condition and who he was. Very little was known about treating these children in the school environment at that time. Jim was lucky, though. He had one good friend in class that always stood by him. It seemed Jim's teacher dealt with his disruptive behavior by having the class ignore him. She isolated him from class activities. He could not go to the bathroom when the other students went as a group. He couldn't get a drink of water with the rest of the class. Jim was devastated. He had no idea how to cope until his friend came up with a plan. When Jim raised his hand to go to the bathroom or the teacher let him go on his own to get a drink of water, he would raise his hand and ask the teacher if he could be excused because he had to go as well. Jim's friend always made sure that my son never left the classroom alone. He was always there to be his backup. He was Jim's best friend and protector.

The principal concluded that if Jim's teacher and I met, we could come to a compatible agreement on what would be best for everyone. So I drove to the school that day to keep my appointment. I no sooner pulled up in the parking lot when my son, who was apparently waiting for me, dashed out of the school building and grabbed my arm as I got out of my car.

"Boy, Mom, am I glad you're here. My teacher and the principal are waiting for you. I will wait for you in my classroom, okay?"

"Okay, honey," I reassured him.

The principal's office was quiet, and she conducted the meeting with Jim's teacher and me as comfortably as she could. Jim's teacher appeared to be on trial here and began her accusations like a lawyer in a courtroom. I just sat and listened as she spurted out her angry accusations toward my son's behavior. When she finished, I slowly looked her way, smiled, and asked one question: "Ma'am, are you married?"

"Yes, I am," she replied.

"Do you have children?"

"No," she answered. "My husband and I can't have children," she reluctantly stated.

"Oh, I see. Well, in that case, would you mind some parental advice?"

"Like what?" she asked.

"Well, as you know, Jim does have a learning disability, and he is on medication. He is trying but cannot always behave the way the other children do. You may want to try to understand his problem and work with him and me. He has one close friend. Why don't you let him be your liaison with Jim? I know it will be frustrating for you at times, but at least try to support him rather than punish him. If you have any problems, just call me and let me know. I will work with you and try to be helpful to Jim in your classroom."

It was hard for her, but we agreed on this approach for a while. After Jim's teacher left the room, the principal confided that she thought things had gone well and Jim's teacher would probably be able to handle him better now that she knew she could always call me for the support she was looking for.

Jim and I left school and drove home. I thought about my conversation with the school principal, and I was grateful that the school had her. She was a friend to the students and the parents as well.

All through Jim's middle school years he had challenges. Some of the students would call him stupid or retarded. And when there was no name-calling, there was the pressure of acceptance by the students. His best friends were his brother and sisters. They would not tolerate anyone who belittled Jim.

One day, Julie came home with the most disappointing story about Jim and one of his classmates. It seemed the class bully was having fun belittling him. He would shove, push, and name call to get him angry. Now, my Jim was a pretty tall and strong man in middle school. But he was also meek and laid back. He never wanted to throw attention his way. This kid kept calling him stupid and retarded until his sister couldn't stand it anymore and complained to me about it.

So when Jim came home from school, I pulled him aside and asked him why he didn't take up for himself against this bully.

"Mom, if I do that, I will be suspended," he blurted out.

"Do you know what that means, Jim?"

"What?" he asked.

"That means you don't have to go to school for two whole days."

"Oh!" He got excited then.

"I want you to start taking up for yourself and let this kid know you mean business. And don't worry about being suspended. There are a lot worse things. Start standing up for yourself, and then maybe the kids will start leaving you alone if they know you won't put up with it."

"Okay, Mom, I'll try."

Pat Karem-Gramig

The next day after school, Julie rushed home and yelled, "Mom! You should have seen Jim today. I was so proud of him. This same bully who is always giving him a hard time came up to Jim and started calling him retarded and poking him in the face. Then Jim turned on him like gang-busters, took him by the collar, and slammed him up against the wall. He yelled at him that if he ever called him retarded again he was going to knock his lights out! Mom, you should have seen this boy. Jim had him pinned up on the wall, and the whole time his feet were dangling like a rag doll. Jim was awesome, Mom! I was so proud of him!"

"Did he get in trouble with the school authorities?" I inquired nervously.

"No, Mom! They were all cool! I think they knew this kid got what he deserved, and they never bothered Jim."

At that moment, I knew my son had become a man.

The Getaway Car

Brian had just turned fifteen and couldn't wait until he could drive. I hardly had the strength to fight him on this issue, and it seemed an everlasting battle. I kept reminding him that he had to be sixteen, and he thought the whole government system was nuts because he wanted to drive now. He just knew he was capable.

It was about 2:00 a.m. when my phone rang and woke me up from a comfortable sleep.

"Hello," I muttered.

"Ms. Karem? This is the police department in Shepherdsville, and we have your sons, Brian and Jim, with us."

"No, you don't," I replied.

"Yes, we do, ma'am. Why don't you check out their bedrooms? I'll wait."

I put the phone down and ran to the boys' bedrooms. Both rooms were empty. I ran back to the phone.

"What are their names?"

"I just told you. Brian James and James Patrick."

"Yes, that's them all right. What did they do?"

"Well, your son Brian was pulled over for a burnt-out tail light. When the officer gave him a warning, he was suspicious of his age and asked for his driver's license. He started to cry, and the policeman brought him in to the police station. We also impounded your car."

Then I got angry. "You don't have my car!"

"Ma'am, look out your driveway and tell me if your car is there."

I dropped the phone again and ran to the living room and looked out my picture window. No car.

"Yes, you have my car. Now what do you want me to do?"

"Ma'am, your son is fifteen. Boys that age think they can get behind the wheel of a car before they legally can. It's normal! We will keep your boys here at the courthouse till you pick them up. They will be safe."

"Well, officer, you have impounded my one and only car. How am I supposed to get there?"

"Ma'am, do you have a neighbor or relative who can bring you?"

"Let me see if I can get someone, and I will be out to get them tomorrow morning."

"Yes, ma'am, that will be fine. I will tell you also that he will have to go before the judge tomorrow to make restitution. The judge is a fair man and will try to impress upon him how serious this could have been for him. There will be nothing else but a scolding by him. Now your son Jim Pat was only a passenger and is not really in any trouble. Would you like to speak to him?"

"Yes, I would, please."

"Hi, Mom," Jim said.

"What happened, Jim?" I asked.

"Brian wanted to buy some fireworks for the Fourth of July, and he wanted to drive to Tennessee because you could get them cheaper there."

"What? Tennessee!" I yelled back.

"Yeah, and he was too chicken to go alone. So he made me go with him. We stopped off at the White Castle to get some hamburgers and started for Nashville. We drove a long time, and then he got worried because it looked like we weren't going to get back before you woke up. So we turned back and started home when we were pulled over by a cop. When he got curious about Brian's age, he made him get out of the car, and when he didn't have a driver's license, he made him lean up against the car and started to frisk him. Mom, you should have seen Brian. He started crying and yelling for you! That's when the cop brought us here."

I told him not to worry and I would see him in the morning. I said good night to my son and made arrangements with a neighbor to take me to pick up the boys. The judge was very understanding but definite. He told them that they now had a record and the next time they got into trouble they would really be going to jail.

Needless to say, my sons got a real sense of justice that day. And I got my family and my car back in one piece.

Not the End

My son Jim grew up to become a wonderful man in spite of his differences. Maybe it's those same differences that make us who we become. Jim was special, unique, and loving. He had more heart than money. He really cared about people, and he cared about his job, wife, children, and his faith. He also served ten years in the air force. When he left the military, he earned the title of sergeant and the good conduct medal, among others. His greatest love of all besides his family was the University of Kentucky. How he loved sports. They kept him alive. They kept him involved. He was a giver, never a taker. He gave his loyalty, trust, and sincere effort in everything he did. What more can you ask of any man? I can think of nothing.

The pain of losing a loved one is always compensated by the love they leave behind. My son left me his two boys. So I think he left me the greatest love of all. I will always miss him, but he is always with me through them.

Epilogue: Mrs. Doubtfire, I Presume?

When all is said and done, parenthood has only one reward. Hopefully, each parent will get their chance to receive it. And that is to be around long enough to witness a great and productive, outstanding human being that they have been responsible for most of their growing up years. Their children.

Robin Williams—what a guy! His performances on the screen are an earmark for living. Robin gave a beautiful performance in Patch Adams. Based on a true story, a doctor proved that a part of healing is caring through humor. Robin proved quite successfully how humor can make a difference in a person's life. Again, humor and love are what it's all about in life.

When the movie Mrs. Doubtfire came out, again I was impressed with Robin Williams's performance. I still am. Not only is he a very polished comedian but also an excellent serious actor, as well. He may be a little off the wall with his comedic content sometimes, but he is a genius in my book. I am sure he has conflict in his personal life. All geniuses do. We, the average persons, never seem to be able to measure up to their level of talent and understanding. That's what makes them special. Anyway, if you haven't seen Mrs. Doubtfire, let me give you a brief synopsis.

It deals with a man who loves his children so much he will do anything to be near them after he loses custody of them during a bitter divorce. He's a very talented actor but has difficulty holding a job due to his free spirit. His brother, a makeup artist, comes to his rescue, and he manages to transform him into an English nanny who takes a position in his children's home without their knowledge. His newfound identity eventually becomes a famous celebrity at a local TV station where he hosts a children's education program that eventually goes nationwide. At the end of the movie, he reads a letter from one of his children viewers who tenderly asks Mrs. Doubtfire the following: "Mrs. Doubtfire, my mommy and daddy are getting a divorce, and my brother says we are losing our family. Is this true?"

Mrs. Doubtfire's response was so touching that it has stayed with me. Mrs. Doubtfire's reply was simple: "Don't be afraid, my dear. Just because your mommy and daddy don't love each other anymore doesn't mean they don't love you. Sometimes, when mommies and daddies don't get along, the family can be a much better family when they live apart. Some families have mommies and daddies that marry again, and then you have two families with two mommies or daddies. And sometimes, dear, it may be an uncle, grandmother, or just a dear friend who loves you. But when you have love, dear, those are the ties that bind. Don't worry, little poppet. You will be all right! Much love, Mrs. Doubtfire."

Her last comment to her little viewer left an impacting message: Each of us lives through many experiences during our lifetimes. Some of them will be good, and some of them will be bad. That's life, a rollercoaster of emotions. But like Mrs.

Doubtfire says, "When you have love, dear, those are the ties that bind."

Sergeant James P. Karem

Cris & Conner Karem (front)
Debra & Jim Karem (back)

Pat Karem-Gramig

Reflections

A peek into memory's window
tells me you are near.
I can see your love reflected there.
The daisies on the window pane
answer my wish to be with you
and I will be, as long as they remain.

I've learned much from your reflection.
It tells me how far I've grown
to meet the sun's opinion
of myself. Do you not feel its
warmth encouraging?
Like you, it has given me
hope for another day.

When the fresh spring air passes
through and winter sheds
her snowy coat from us, I will
think of those daisies
and how lovely they became
when they reached up and
kissed the moments they
shared with that window.

—Pat Karem

Afterword: Lost Children

If your heart is in the right place, your head will soon follow.

Every day when I get on my computer, I have dozens of e-mails from the local Families for Early Autism Treatment (FEAT) group, a support group for those families that have children with some form of autism. It is like reading an ongoing mystery drama. I read each and every one of these for my own self-education.

Each e-mail is usually written by the mothers of these children, and they carry a scary truth about them. If they are not searching for a good doctor, they are constantly dealing with problems that they want to resolve so their child can function normally in this world, such as, "I need to locate a school for my child that will support him with a special needs program," or, "I am looking for a special diet that my child needs in order to reduce the risk of his type of behavior," or, "Do you know of a nanny or sitter that is trained in dealing with an autistic child?" or, how about this one, "I can't seem to get the government to cooperate by creating a good and workable bill that will support the special needs of our autistic children."

Some of these problems refer to the types of medication or treatment they are receiving and how these children cannot function without proper support. It seems each parent who deals with these situations becomes his or her own medical advisor. They are constantly struggling to make it a better world for their child.

I also read between the lines of these struggling parents. And what I am reading is the neverending battle of fatigue, frustration, and unlimited spirit these parents have. Do you realize how much courage it takes to deal with these types of situations on a daily basis? And here is another scary part of this problem. Some of these families are dealing with more than one child who has this disorder. I just don't know how they do it. The struggle of these parents, though, does make a difference.

I am sure my son had a form of this social disorder, but when we had him evaluated at the age of five, there was very little knowledge or research about autism. I did the best I could with what was available back then.

Now I am dealing with this disorder at a much higher level than before. But the frustration and fatigue and the endless and tiring effort to help these boys remains the same. I can sympathize with the pain and anguish a parent feels dealing with the daily struggles. Each day brings on a different challenge, and each day carries you through another educational process. You never stop learning, and you never stop fighting a new challenge. And it is always very exhausting.

Did I not mention a creativity element here as well? All parents definitely become creative in accomplishing the impossible. My husband and I placed our grandchildren in the Boy Scout Program (they always go on these functions with their grandfather, who is an Eagle Scout). They took Tae Kwon Do lessons with me. They are black tips, and I am a brown belt, and, I might add, the oldest student there, but I managed to keep up. They attend a regular school that provides them with the counselors and teachers who are aware of their disorder. Their progress there is due to the diligence, patience, and understanding of the teaching staff. Both boys are active on the academic team, orchestra, band, and even the drama club. I'm not saying that we do not have our problems from time to time. But what I am saying is that when a problem does occur, the outcome has a far more positive effect on everyone involved, including the students, teachers, and family members. They are educated about differences, and they become better people due to this. Because of this teamwork effort, Conner graduated from the eighth grade as an A-B student and is now in his junior year in high school. He has played the violin for seven years and has been a member of the school orchestras. Cris is in to his sophomore year. He has played the clarinet for five years with school bands. Conner's goal is to join the FBI and work with the research team. Cris wants to become a doctor, and both boys are now working toward their Eagle Badge in the Scout program. They both have more than thirty-five merit badges. They both are members of the Boy Scouts "Order of the Arrow," an honorary organization.

We also put them in the Big Brother program after their father died, the best thing we ever did. We have them in the Star Foundation for additional therapy and periodic physical evaluations. Their pediatrician monitors their growth stages and monitors their medications as they continue to grow. I love their pediatrician at the Star Foundation. Dr. Patricia Gail Williams is a very patient, kind, and caring doctor. She is always there for us when we need her. Grace Mathai, their counselor at the Star Foundation, was instrumental in helping us through their father's death with grief counseling. She continued to work with them as they entered their teens with counseling on how to better socialize and how to relate better to the outside world. She, too, is a kind and supportive person. Now that they are teenagers with a whole new set of challenges, Grace also formed a group therapy session with all teenage boys. There were about six teens involved. When they were being counseled, the parents would go off into a room on our own and share "war stories" on how we were managing our lives with our guys. When the sessions discontinued, the families decided to stay together and do some fun things with the boys. The boys loved it. They seemed to fit somewhere. I call them the "Star Foundation Gang."

Each of these boys has a special talent. Michael is the Daniel Boone of the group. He is a typical outdoorsman. He loves to fish. And his mother takes him fishing almost every day. He knows everything about fishing, bait, rods, reels, and the best places to fish. He can name just about every fish in existence. Anything he catches, he cleans and scales. When he hunts squirrel, dove, turtle, and other small game, he guts them, skins, and butchers them. When it comes to deer, though, his mother claims he prefers the packinghouse do the dirty work for him. Then after the packinghouse has his deer butchered, he prepares the meat with his own personal marinating sauce for cooking. And he does all the cooking. Michael is only fourteen years old, but I told Michael if there was ever a global war, I want to be with him. I know we could survive with his special talents. Michael and my grandson Cris have one thing in common. They both love fishing!

Evan is more involved with sports. He and Conner share this special talent. Evan is sixteen years old, and so is Conner. Both are loners and somewhat shy, but not when it comes to sports; this is where they thrive. They both have a special team in baseball, and you can tell this when they start talking about their favorite team. They beam from ear to ear. But both boys know about every team in every sports category. When Evan is around the other boys, he opens up and begins to share conversation. So does Conner. Both fit in and are more comfortable.

The youngest of the teenage therapy group is twelve, and his name is Matthew. I know very little about his family, but what I have seen when he attends the sessions with his mom and sister, Caroline, is quite heartwarming. He has an anger management problem just like Conner. His mom says that this causes the other children to fear him at times. His sister, who is in high school, is something to see when she is with him. You can tell that her young brother adores her and she adores him. She is very loving and patient with him, and each week when the sessions end, she gently picks him up and carries him on her back all the way to the parking lot. I asked him what he wanted to be when he grew up, and he said, "I want to be a scientist and discover a cure for Asperger's." I believe him.

There is not much known about our last teenager of the group. All I know is that he is seventeen, has a gentle manner, and a very sweet smile. His mother works, so he gets anywhere he needs to be by bus. When he finished school for the day, he would wait and take the bus to the other end of town where our counseling sessions were held. We offered to pick him up from school and bring him with us, but he quietly said that he would have to check with his mom. He wasn't able to attend many of the classes, but he was missed. I think he is planning to attend a special college in the fall.

I learned this much from all these different processes. Things never remain the same. Nor does your child. They need constant monitoring and constant challenging. They need to develop, and they can't do that without the proper tools. It takes everybody's teamwork efforts to accomplish this.

Ignorance can be a dangerous thing. When Asperger children begin attending school and try to learn to associate with other children, the bullying issue plays a hand at their educational and emotional future. There was a small amount of bullying in the primary and secondary grades with Cris and Conner, but when they entered high school, it became more obvious, more often and brutal at times. We were able to work through most of it, but in Conner's junior year, the bullying issue began to take its toll on his patience. Both boys rode the school bus, and most of it occurred there with a few troublesome students. One day, the name calling and being ridiculed in public finally took Conner over the edge. He caused no problems on the school bus, but his anger was building.

When the school bus drops off its passengers, the students must stay in the cafeteria until the first class bell rings. It was there that Conner could no longer take the abuse. So he took his anger out on a metal poster and easel in the school hall. He punched it, and it crumbled to the ground in tiny pieces. He was suspended for this. The school has a no-tolerance policy so when the incident occurred, they were unaware what had provoked him to act in this manner. Nor were they aware of his social disorder. They took immediate measures to control Conner, who had gotten out of hand and destroyed school property. We were devastated over this, but Conner accepted his punishment like a man, for he realized that he had taken his anger out in the wrong way. He knew the difference between right and wrong. So, during his suspension, he came to me with a determined look and announced, "Mommo, I may as well be doing something more productive while I am home for these next six days. I need to do some community service to get my next merit badge in scouts, so I am going to call the Wayside Christian Mission and donate my time while I am home."

My heart filled with pride. Where did my Asperger teenager go? It suddenly dawned on me that Conner had finally connected and learned to manage a bad situation. This was encouraging to me since I knew that if he approached any future bullying issues within the school environment in this same controlled manner, he would be better prepared to deal with any obstacle that confronted him in the real world. I was now talking to a sensible young man. When he made this suggestion, I mentioned that he might want to include Rich, his Big Brother, to go with him. Conner thought that was a great idea. So he contacted Rich and then Wayside. It was settled. Both went to Wayside and served meals to the needy. Conner got his merit badge, Rich got some bonding time with Conner, and I witnessed Conner's next level of maturity.

Another good thing came from this incident. and that involved Conner's brother, Cris. Cris is a very non-violent individual and more socially outgoing that his brother. He likes to be liked by everyone and sometimes makes bad choices selecting his friends. In fact, some of Cris's so-called friends were responsible for bullying Conner on the school bus. I am assuming that was their way to alienate Cris from his brother in order to control him into doing what they wanted him to do. When Cris witnessed firsthand the results from making bad choices, the impact was very rewarding. He and his brother became closer than they already were. He severed his relationships from his troublesome friends and devoted more time to his studies and family and church. He wanted to avoid communicating with them on Facebook, so he requested, on his own, for me to confiscate his laptop and his PSP. He wanted no part of the troublemakers who threatened his family. It seemed that he too was trying to become a more mature teenager. He and his Big Brother, Dominique, began planning more constructive things together, such as community projects with the Wayside Christian Mission and attending more church activities at his Big Brother's church as well as his own. In essence, the Big Brother Program was supporting our efforts with the boys in a very significant way. This kind of progress only emphasizes the importance of family over fair-weather friends. The moral of this story? Don't mess with family, faith, or morals. It won't do you any good. We win out in the end anyway, as long as we stick together. And I guarantee you we will.

My husband and I also partnered in this new alliance with the boys. We made sure that the boys were alienated from the bullies on the school bus. We drove them to and from school each day. Conner and Cris started visiting the library before the first bell, rather than the cafeteria. Conner promised Cris that if his old friends tried to bother him, he would be there to make sure they didn't, but Cris had to learn to deal with this on his own. Conner would only be there for moral support. Cris felt good about that. We all learned a good lesson in family bonding and what makes a difference in the way we make choices.

Prior to this incident, Conner's English teacher had given her class an essay assignment. It was a personal profile that each student was required to do. When Conner finished the assignment, he asked me to check his punctuation and his spelling for him. So I did. When I read his paper, I was so deeply moved that I felt the bullying issue his father experienced when he was Conner's age was being repeated now, through his son. I also felt that he too had become a man just like his dad. On that note, I want to share his essay with you so you can make your own conclusions about feelings, integrity, and how an Asperger child can make a difference when ignorance tries to take charge.

The Abnormal Child
By Conner Karem

Every day I walk through the halls at school dodging the other students, excited about the start of a new day of learning. As I walk through the halls, I become mentally challenged. "How?" you may ask. I become stronger by listening to all the negative comments about my personality, my clothes, and my looks. But I understand why I get teased a lot. You see, the kids really don't know or understand me. I have a form of autism. I was born with Aspberger's Syndrome, which is a social disorder that is sometimes very challenging for me. The reason for this is I am a very independent person. If I am around a lot of people, I get very shy and I stay more to myself. I like to eat alone, and I want to be left alone some of the time. That is what a social disorder IS! When I do talk to people, I never look the person in the eye. I guess it is because I'm not very comfortable talking to the other person. But, if someone does talk to me, I'll talk in a low voice, and sometimes the kids don't understand me.

Most of the time, I just can't handle it. But no matter what happens, any challenge that may come my way will make me stronger if I keep trying.

The other thing that the other kids don't know about me is that I am 100% functional. I am just like you. I like and do certain things that help me grow, just like you. For instance:

I am a Star Scout in the Boy Scouts. My brother and I are members of Troop 1, which is the third oldest troop in the United States. I am proud of that. I am also a member of the Order of the Arrow, which is a sacred and secret fraternity of the Boy Scouts. Soon, I will be working on my Eagle Scout badge, which is the highest honor you can achieve. It will help me open doors to school scholarship opportunities for college. I am also a Black Tip in Tae Kwon Do. I studied this martial art to learn to focus better and to help me with my coordination. I studied for two years with my brother and my grandmother, who is a brown belt. You better not mess with her!

I played the violin in the school orchestra for seven years. Last year I went to Disney

World in Florida with the orchestra. It was a good experience for me, and I made some good friendships in the orchestra while I was there. After my dad died three years ago, I was placed in the Big Brother/Big Sister Program. I now have a big brother that I hang out with and go to a lot of sports functions with. I love sports! In fact, you can call me a sports fanatic. So as you can see, I am really involved in a lot of things.

If you still don't understand or know me, then I challenge you to educate yourself about Asperger's. Find out more about it. I challenge you to go to your local library and look for books about Asperger's, I challenge you to go online and look up information about Asperger's and take some quality time reading this information. Not only will you be able to understand me better, but also other kids with similar disorders.

All I need, or anyone needs for that matter, is the love and support of friends and more importantly, family. If people gave me the same respect as they do their other friends, they will find that I'm a really nice guy. But unfortunately, as the hot band Green Day always says, "Nice guys finish last."

If teachers and students took the time to know and better understood kids like me, maybe we wouldn't have so many kids commit suicide every year. Kids today can be mean. When someone tells me that I need to shut up because I didn't know what I was talking about and that I'm the weirdest person in the whole school, I know that I can be a much better and stronger person in spite of these types of remarks. If it weren't for my family and my counselors at the Star Foundation, I wouldn't be able to handle what I can today. I always stop and wonder, "What if there is more that I could do? But I know that what I'm doing is all I can do, for now. Whatever comes my way, I know it will make me a stronger person and a better man—a real man. I know I will have my struggles, but no matter the challenges that lie ahead for me, I will always wake up in the morning knowing I am not ashamed of who I am. In my opinion, it's what makes me special.

What Conner wrote here, says it all.

There is still one other underlying issue on this subject that needs to be addressed. That issue is the caretaker. Yes, this can be an issue if the caretaker is not considered. The caretaker is the person who manages, encourages, teaches, researches, and continues to love their child at all levels of their development. The caretaker has to have certain credentials. They have to have patience, understanding, faith, tenacity, a good support team, an investigative personality, a good sense of humor, and most importantly, personal private time. A long list of strong credentials, don't you think? Caring for these children can be emotionally draining. In the small support group that I belong to, I can see how the only drive these women have is the love they have for their child; the constant drive to try to make things better for them.

I get a lot of emails from NAA (National Autistic Association), and each year they have a conference for caretakers. This year it was in Florida. I read the agenda and the list consisted of speakers who were qualified doctors, technicians, counselors, and even authors. The litany of excellence was exciting for me to read. I was dying to go. It would give me some private time and yet network with others who had their own experiences and points of view, and I wanted to connect with these people. My point is, caretakers in any category, not just in the Asperger category, must find some time to rejuvenate. Caretakers are special too and need to take care of themselves so they are better able to take care of others.

My private time is early in the morning. I am an early riser, and I love the peace and quiet. It gives me time to think through my day and it is also my best time to write. My thoughts are refreshed and focused with clarity. I am me! My other private moment is walking. I love to walk. So after the boys are off to school, I walk my neighborhood with a fast pace. I try to walk two miles every morning. At my age, I consider that a pretty exceptional feat. But it is my time. It makes me happy. So a caretaker needs to find what makes him or her happy, peaceful, and content. Caretakers have a big job to do, and in order to accomplish this, peace and contentment should be their support system.

Slowly there is a small glimmer of hope, though, and the realization that with proper education and support, these children's needs are being met. We need to meet these needs and understand these children. As their caretaker, I tell my grandkids all the time that they are special. They are bright and uniquely different. Their special talents could benefit our society in the near future. Maybe even in my lifetime. And who knows? That difference might create for all of us a better future. I think as a society we are starting to listen to them. Well, it's about time!

What Is Asperger's Syndrome

Its name is derived from its founder, an Austrian pediatrician, Dr. Hans Asperger. In 1944, he described children in his practice that lacked nonverbal communication skills, demonstrated limited empathy with their peers, and were physically clumsy. Fifty years later, it was standardized as a diagnosis, but many questions remain about aspects of the disorder.

It is a social disorder, not a disability. Asperger's can be managed so that the person who has this disorder can be totally aware of what it is and how they can manage it in order to live a productive life. This, of course, takes time, repetition, a lot of patience, and most of all, a lot of love. As a child with Asperger's grows and matures into adulthood, the challenges are still there but in a more adult form. That is why the development of this child is pretty much like any other child. It just takes a different road of education. Most people who have this social disorder have a very high IQ, and some of their idiosyncrasies develop into a very powerful talent. I have seen this to be true.

Asperger children's brains communicate at a different level. Everything they hear is interpreted literally by the brain. They do not totally understand that our language and our words have more than one meaning. They do not totally understand abstract forms of words like idioms. They are only focused on one definition.

I will give you an example: Many teenagers today will use the expression, "Oh, get out of here!" They usually use this phrase when they are awed over a statement or a claim that is made. They just can't believe their ears when they hear something "totally awesome!" So they use this expression. But when you say this in front of an Asperger child, he will leave the room.

Here is another example: There is a two-letter word that has many meanings. This word is *up*. When you look up the word *up* in the dictionary, it is used as an adverb, preposition, adjective, noun, or verb—a lot of ways to use this small word. And, yet, it can be very confusing to an Asperger child.

It is easy to understand up, meaning toward the sky or at the top of the list, but when we awaken in the morning, we wake up. At a meeting, a topic comes up. We speak up. Officials are up for an election. We write up a report. We clean up the kitchen. People stir up trouble. To be knowledgeable about the proper uses of up, we have to review about thirty definitions of a two-letter word.

This in itself is a challenge to parents as well as teachers. You have to learn a new way to communicate with your child. I compare it to someone speaking Spanish to a Frenchman. We have to learn to translate our thoughts in a way that our child will understand. Can you imagine a whole classroom of children with differences and the teacher has to communicate so all will understand? I have learned to give teachers and counselors a great deal of respect and a lot more of my understanding. They have the most difficult job of all. I just don't know how they do it.

Some Asperger children have other special hidden talents. That is what I tell my grandsons. God gave them special talents, and it is up to us to develop them and learn how to manage them so they can become the best leaders this world has ever experienced. These children are our future.

Some of these children are tuned into sound. They are sensitive to noise. A dripping water facet or the hum of a motor from a drinking fountain can freak them out. Some children are magnificent repairmen. They can look at a broken piece of mechanism and know how to put it back together again. My daughter-in-law's nephew does this. He is only seven years old, and when he comes to my home, he is always asking questions about how things work. Then if he finds something broken, he wants to fix it. He also loves to watch and turn the drum of the clothes washer. He is fascinated by its rotation.

Some Asperger children approach life through feeling and colors. I read a book about an Asperger savant child. He could perform extraordinary calculations in his head. He learned to speak new languages fluently from scratch within a week. He memorized and recited more than twenty-two thousand digits of pi, setting a record. He associated his words and feelings through colors, touch, and textures. When he grew up, he wrote his memoirs, entitled Born on a Blue Day. It took my breath away. It taught me that anything is possible when you keep trying. Defeat is a word that describes quitting. Quitting kills one's inspiration to challenge. No one gets anywhere when they quit. Today, this man runs his own successful web-based business for language tutorials.

Speaking of language experts here, I would like to share a story about another individual that had this type of expertise, as well. My stepfather, Harry, is an amazing man. He is eighty-three years old and comes from a family of thirteen children. Our nation was experiencing difficult economic times when he was a boy. He and his siblings lived in a small house with their mother. There was always food to eat, maybe not much, but as Harry says, his mom always knew how to find that extra dollar whenever they needed it. I believe he mentioned a "sugar bowl in the pantry" technique.

When World War II broke out in 1941, just about everything our country produced was being rationed for the cause of the war. Three years later, at the age of fifteen, Harry decided to accomplish more with his life, so he joined the merchant marines with his mother's permission. He was assigned to Liberty ships that cruised the Atlantic and Pacific. There were three different ships he was assigned to before the war ended. He always talked about working hard, eating well, and watching the enemy torpedoes cut through the waters near by. He later said that, looking back, he had no idea of the real dangers he was facing at that time. He was just too young to capture the full impact of the tragedies of war.

One of the better things that developed from his military career was that he received an education he probably wouldn't have gotten on his own. Harry's career progressed to the Army Intelligence unit. He became friends with many interesting people and one very unusual man. This man was a quiet person, never said much to anyone, but he had the ability to understand and translate as many as seven different languages into English without any special training. He was able to accomplish this quickly with the speed of Superman on a manual typewriter using the two-finger method and without missing a stroke. The man was a genius.

Even though he was so talented in this specialized field, he was not capable of tying his combat boots with all the lace-ups or making his bed. This just seemed to be more difficult for him to figure out. Combat boots do not stand up tall. No, they lean over to either side of the boot in a limped position when you're not wearing them. He was always late for inspection for not being able to perform these simple army tasks. So Harry and the commanding officer thought if they would put paper in his boots, they would stand up straighter. Then all he needed to do was to jump out of bed, put on his socks, ease right into his boots, and lace them up without any trouble. So they tried this. The next morning, he arrived for inspection on time, all right, but the paper was still in his boots, along with his socks and feet. He was not able to think through the process of removing the paper after he got his feet into the boots. Asperger's syndrome? Maybe, maybe not. Yes, he was different, but in such a special, talented way. And the thing of it is, the army recognized this when he was a recruit and used his special talent to enable the army to become better equipped to handle intelligence work through this fine translator. So you see, these special talents can make a difference. And these differences can definitely fit into society somewhere, somehow. We just need to think it through the process like the paper in the boots.

What Asperger's has meant to me is to respect the differences in all of us. Key word here: respect. Read about Asperger's. Learn more about it, and the knowledge you seek and find awards you a newfound respect for the differences in all people. Asperger's syndrome is no different from any other disease or disorder. It just needs to be understood by more of us. Ignorance is the disease here.

Whenever I engage in a conversation with someone about Asperger's, there always seems to be the same question asked of me: "How long has this been around? How come I've never heard of it before?"

I don't know. But I do know this: North America was always here. It took a few brave men believing in a dream to discover it. Now look what we've become: a nation of great possibilities. I guess we have to go search and discover our hopes and dreams to realize a great truth. We are constantly discovering new ways through research to uncover truth with any disease or any disorder. Just because we don't know it exists doesn't mean it's not there.

I also know from personal experience that the genetic factor is much a part of Asperger's syndrome. It is also complicated with other factors as well. Some children who have Asperger's also have a form of Tourette Syndrome, ADHD, ADD, or bipolar disorder. That is why you should check on the family genetic background. If you even suspect that your child may have some sort of disorder, you should do the following as soon as you can:

- Early Testing: If you or a family member has a history of any kind of disorder and you suspect your child may also have these tendencies, get your child tested as early as possible. The earlier you discover a problem, the better it is for your child. If you don't know where to go, check out medical websites such as Web MD. This website contains a wealth of information on numerous illnesses and disorders. There are several additional sources of information that are also helpful in your search. They are: the Center for Communicative Diseases in Atlanta (www.cdc.gov). This source is excellent with solid scientific information on autism; the Autism Society of America (www.autismsociety.org), and Autism Speaks (www.autismspeaks.org). The Autism Society of America and Autism Speaks are two parent-centered organizations that are among the very best places for information and support. Or ask your physician. But do something.

- Find a Support Group: There are many local support groups that offer knowledge, funding, and even inform you of legislation that is happening in your local and state government. Take the time to educate yourself to these. If you don't know where to find them, contact the NAA (National Autism Association) and FEAT (Families for Effective Autism Treatment) and my favorite resource, STAR (Systamatic Treatment of Autism and Related Disorders). This foundation is associated with the Weisskopf Child Evaluation Center through the University of Louisville. You will be surprised at the good, solid information that is there for you.

- Ongoing Testing: As your child develops, so will his differences. Do not quit on your child when it comes to testing him physically and emotionally. He is just like you in this manner. Regular checkups will help you monitor his growth potential, and if something changes during his development, you have his past history that will enable you to improve his future needs.

- Attend conferences that will educate you: My husband and I were fortunate to run across a conference that was being conducted by Dr. Manuel Casanova, associate chair for research at U of L. The conference was basically for medical people, but it was open free to the public. It was being conducted at the Jewish hospital downtown, and our grandchildren's pediatrician at the Star Foundation was going to give a portion of the presentation. We immediately signed up. The conference was an all-day event, and we were really excited about the panel. It varied from pediatricians, genetic experts, legal experts who would counsel parents of their children's rights and what to expect regarding insurance benefits, teen counselors who would introduce you to the problems to expect with your Asperger teen, guidance counselors who support the everyday living problems as well as school problems, and legislation experts. It was an amazing conference, and I bragged about it to everyone I knew. I am hoping they will conduct another one and focus toward parents attending. It was so worthwhile.

Everything I have mentioned here is based on a layman's experience and knowledge, firsthand. I am a mom whose middle son probably had Asperger's syndrome, but he slipped through the cracks of scientific research. I am also a grandmother with two grandsons who have this disorder, possibly just like their father. I also have eleven other grandchildren who are just downright feisty. I am no medical expert by any means. But parents do have an insight that only comes from living experiences. You need both. Do not fear the unknown. Challenge it to the best of your ability, and you will always come out the winner. I have living proof: my two living testimonials that prove anything is possible.

If you haven't guessed already, I am addicted to this newfound disorder. It surprises me more every day how unique and yet how similar this disorder is to each and every one of us. I truly believe we all have a little of Asperger's syndrome within us.

When my husband and I were first told about Conner and Cris having this disorder, I immediately went to the bookstore and picked out the most recently published book. We bought others, but in time, I developed my favorites. I would like to list them here for you just in case you haven't researched anything on your own yet.

Asperger's Syndrome & Your Child: This is a parent's guide to unlocking your child's potential. It is written by Michael D. Powers, PSY.D, and Janet Poland, a coauthor of several other parenting books.

When Conner and Cris started in middle school, I approached the counselors there and told them that their homework assignment was to read about this disorder so they could get better acquainted with my grandchildren. Counselors did not have it in their school budget to purchase too many of these books, so I started buying them some, and they all took turns copying pages from the book to read on sections that interested them. They actually began their own small library that was supervised by the main counselor.

Different Like Me: This book is not very thick. But it goes in detail about many famous people who were a little different and possibly had some of the symptoms of autism and Asperger's syndrome. Each of these famous people mentioned in the book carried a brief story about their lives and challenges. They are Albert Einstein, Sir Isaac Newton, Andy Kaufman, Hans Christian Anderson, and among many others, the famous Dr. Temple Grandin, who is a noted autistic, author, speaker, an American doctor of animal science, and a professor at Colorado State University. She is a great role model for autistic people all over the world.

When I first purchased this book, I would sit at the breakfast table each morning and read to Conner and Cris about one of these famous people. I wanted them to know that it was a good thing to be different. I wanted them to learn how to feel good about themselves and how important it is to be uniquely different. I wanted them to learn that they can accomplish anything. But they have to try regardless what others may think. It is more important what they thought about themselves.

Born on a Blue Day: This is the memoir of Daniel Tammet. He had an extraordinary mind of an autistic savant. He evaluated our language with numbers, colors, and textures. For example, the number nine made him feel intimidated. So he associated that number with that word. This is an amazing book to read. It is a memoir of a young man who is a savant and faces the challenges of Asperger's Syndrome, epilepsy, and phobias. With the help of his family and doctors, he becomes a very successful and productive human being and businessman.

The Dream Manager: My daughter Diane told me about this book. It has nothing to do with autism or Asperger's, but I guarantee you it has everything to do with life. It talks about dreams. Growth and success in anything you do is built on dreams—your life, your business, your family, and even your disorder. Before I purchased this book, and without knowing its content, I made a screensaver for my computer. Every day, it scrolls across my screen with this message: "Live your dreams…and you will become the person you choose to be."

I never realized how close to the truth I was with that message until I purchased this book. Get yourself a dream book. It's worth it.

The Velveteen Rabbit: Another classic book that needs to be read. Again, it has nothing to do with autism. Or does it? Read it, and especially take time to read the passage when the velveteen rabbit asks the question, "What is real?" It is one of my favorite books to read.

Now that I've given you some basics about Asperger's, it is up to you to take this information and fly with it. There are no limitations, only aspirations. Good luck, and show no fear. You are never alone. So hang in there! The parents of Asperger children of the world are with you always.

Conner Karem
Violinist, High School Orchestra

Cris and Conner
Boy Scouts—Troop 1

About the Author

Pat Karem-Gramig is a liberated woman, single parent, grandmother-parent, great-grandmother, and wife. She was born and raised in Louisville, Kentucky. Her professional background has been in the promotional, public relations, and advertising areas. Her interests over the years involved acting, writing, poetry, playing the classical piano, knitting, and most recently, Tae Kwan Do. She is a brown belt but quips that she is not dangerous. She still jumps on the couch and yells her head off if she spies a mouse (the mouse must be a black belt).

She and her husband, Jerry, are focused on getting better acquainted with autism and especially Asperger's Syndrome and raising Cris and Conner with every opportunity they can provide for them. Pat says she is retired. Well, at least for now she is.

Her Children

Brian J. Karem is an award-winning investigative reporter, writer, producer, veteran, bestselling true crime author, and former correspondent for *America's Most Wanted*. He was the first American reporter allowed inside Pablo Escobar's palatial prison after Escobar's escape from Colombian authorities, and he was one of the first reporters to enter Kuwait City after its liberation during the first Gulf War. A regular contributor to *People* magazine, Mr. Karem has also interviewed James Carville, Mary Matalin, and G. Gordon Liddy for *Playboy*. Mr. Karem was presented with the National Press Club's Freedom of the Press Award after he was jailed for protecting a confidential source in 1992. He lives outside of Washington, D.C., with his wife and three children, Zach, Brennan, and Wyatt. Pam is the only female in the household. Even their dogs are males. Brian is currently the managing editor of the Montgomery County Sentinel. It is the oldest newspaper in the Washington DC area.

Julie, my oldest daughter, is the assistant deli manager and caterer at ValuMarket. She also has an artistic background. Julie was the glue that kept our family together with laughter and love. She and her husband, Manual, have two children,

Matt, who created his own comic book and characters, and Sierra, whose talents cover the gamut.

Diane is the senior account executive of Advertising Vehicles based out of Cincinnati, as well as past president of the Advertising Club of Louisville. She also serves on the board for FEAT. Her daughter, Jessie, is responsible for making me a great-grandmother. Thank you, Jessie!

Jim Pat served in the air force for ten years. When he left the military, he had earned the rank of Sergeant as well as the Good Conduct Medal with "One" Devise, along with a list of other honors and awards. Jim was with the maintenance team at Walmart before he died. They have a plaque honoring him on their wall where he worked.